WALKING BY FAITH:

AN AFRO-AMERICAN

TRILOGY

Revised Edition

*A Dramatic Trilogy Celebrating
Afro-American Accomplishments*

BY

ZERETHA JENKINS

HERE'S WHAT AUTHORS, PROFESSIONALS, RELIGIOUS CLERGY AND THEATRE BUFFS ARE SAYING ABOUT

WALKING BY FAITH: AN AFRO-AMERICAN TRILOGY
Revised Edition

"Zeretha Jenkins is a writer after my own heart. In her Afro-American Trilogy she educates while entertaining and entertains while giving us a history lesson. Her humor keeps you just enough off-kilter to keep you turning pages, or in your seat. It should be a welcome addition to school drama departments as well as to material hungry African-American theatre groups of all stripes."

- *Micki Grant,* **Multiple-Award-Winning Writer, Actor, and Grammy-Winning Composer/ Author/Lyricist of the Broadway Musical,** *Don't Bother Me, I Can't Cope,* **and others**

"My Christian Sister Zeretha has scored again as she uses her playwright genuineness to give insight to the body, mind, and spiritual personality of great African Americans, who have made great contributions to our Black History.

In page after page in these three plays you can see the compassionate, innovative, warm richly talented figure of the author touching the life and thoughts of generations of great leaders who kept the faith and not only talked the talk but walked the walk.

May God bless her as she continues to use her gift in love and faith."

- *Minister Olevia Stewart-Smith, MSW, M.Div. Canaan Baptist Church of Christ, New York, NY*

"In reading *Walking By Faith: An Afro- American Trilogy,* it renewed my spirit and faith. We are a chosen people. Yes, the road has not been easy. *Walking By Faith* clearly confirms our survival.

Thank you, Zeretha, for sharing your God-given gift of pen."
- ***Eleanor Kennedy, Retail Business Owner, Harlem, NY***

"Words – the right words when carefully chosen – are priceless gifts that can inspire, uplift and lead us to greater achievements. *Walking By Faith: An Afro-American Trilogy* does all these things and more. The characters' words, their dialogue, spoken at just the right time are both exciting and enlightening! This book re-ignites the spark within my heart that makes me proud, ever so proud, to be of African ancestry. I strongly advise anyone who is *Walking By Faith* to take this delightful journey!"
- ***Vanessa K. Carroll, Stephen Minister***
Lakewood Church, Houston, TX

"*Walking By Faith: An Afro- American Trilogy* gives a nicely crafted glimpse into the historical contributions of Black Americans and their impact upon the world. This is easy reading but provides a quick and profound flashback on black culture. May it be performed and/or become required reading especially for grade school students."
- ***Gerald Savage, Professor - Essex County College, Newark, NJ***

"Thrilling…humorous…uplifting and educational all at once! *Walking By Faith: An Afro-American Trilogy* stresses a key message: acknowledge your past, and embrace the present so that you can control and mold your destination – your future. Now that I can truly relate to!"
- ***Jovian Terrell, New Orleans, LA***

"These characters will live forever because they so accurately capture the essence of us as Afro-American people."
— ***Vivian Wesley, Reno, Nevada***

"I've never enjoyed a better history lesson! *Walking By Faith: An Afro-American Trilogy* is enlightening, educational, and entertaining."
— ***Terra LaShon, Houston, TX***

"*Walking By Faith: An Afro-American Trilogy* is a grand journey through Afro-American history that has a universal theme for all."
— ***Malik K. Travis, Chicago, IL***

"*Walking By Faith: An Afro-American Trilogy* is a constant inspiration for me and a reminder that our footsteps in life lead from our heritage to any significant goals *we choose to accomplish.*"
— ***Debra A. Hill, Monroe, LA***
Radiologic Technologist

"What a magnificent timely journey you've provided us in *Walking By Faith: An Afro-American Trilogy*. So refreshing, uplifting and entertaining! Thank you!"
— ***Steve Hinton, Atlanta, GA***

"People of all ethnicities, races, colors and classes should see this work performed! It's appropriate 24/7 and is *always in season!*"
— ***Freda J. Hoston, Law Enforcement, Louisiana***

"Thanks for honoring people of African ancestry – especially Afro-Americans – with this trilogy of plays deserving production in America and abroad. It's *both* a *must read* and a *must see!*"
— ***Heather R. Jefferson, Dallas, TX***

"As a writer, I know the immense number of creative elements that must come together to create truly magnificent drama. Zeretha Jenkins has accomplished this and more. *Walking By Faith: An Afro-American Trilogy* is really an amazing work that's great for all age levels. Don't pass up the opportunity to experience this *walk of faith*."

- Karen S. Thornton, Los Angeles, CA

"I've been a Christian almost all of my life and have seen some outstanding religious and inspirational plays in my day. *Walking By Faith: An Afro-American Trilogy* is destined to be such a jewel."

- Gertrude K. Marks, Beaumont, TX

"How refreshing it is to see such a work as *Walking By Faith: An Afro-American Trilogy* that not only accurately presents us as an Afro-American people but also simultaneously educates and entertains. I'd love to see these characters in a sequel. So get to writing!"

- Marvin Singletary, Washington, DC

"I read *Walking By Faith: An Afro-American Trilogy* and could see the universal message in it for all people who've ever encountered struggle. Though its emphasis is on the Afro-American experience, its profound message is that the past, present, and future form the composite of us as human beings. *All three are important* – that's the *universal theme* we must **all** remember lest we allow history to repeat some of its most serious mistakes. Thumbs up! A great work for anyone who shares this philosophy."

- Marcus Orlando, Dallas, TX

"*Walking By Faith: An Afro-American Trilogy* is truly inspirational! It's a timeless piece everyone should read and also see performed."

- Betty S. Hampton, Jacksonville, FL

WALKING BY FAITH:
AN AFRO-AMERICAN TRILOGY

Revised Edition

OTHER BOOKS BY ZERETHA JENKINS

Walking By Faith: An Afro-American Trilogy

Walking By Faith: An Afro-American Trilogy And More

Walking By Faith: Fact Or Fiction

OTHER OFFERINGS BY E.F.S. ONLINE PUBLISHING

The Golden Path of Human Heart

I See The Light

8   Walking By Faith: An Afro-American Trilogy

WALKING BY FAITH: AN AFRO-AMERICAN TRILOGY

Revised Edition

By Zeretha Jenkins

Published and Distributed By
E.F.S. Online Publishing
New York

10 Walking By Faith: An Afro-American Trilogy

Copyright © 1998, 2006 by Zeretha Jenkins. Printed in the United States of America.

All rights, including professional productions, amateur and stock performances, radio, television and internet broadcasting, motion picture, recording, public reading, recitation, lecturing, any type of photographic reproduction, and rights regarding translation into foreign languages, etc., are strictly reserved. Permission regarding professional productions, amateur and stock performances must be secured in writing from E.F.S. Enterprises, Inc., P.O. Box 7605, New York, NY 10116-7605. No part of this book may be reproduced or transmitted in any form or by any means, electronic or mechanical, including photocopying, recording, or by any information storage and retrieval system without written permission from the publisher, except for the inclusion of brief quotations in a review.

Attention corporations, writing organizations, institutions, and conferences: Get a 20% discount when you use our books as fundraisers, gifts, or premiums. For more information on these special offers, please contact the publisher:

E.F.S. Online Publishing
P.O. Box 7605
New York, New York 10116-7605
(212) 283-8899
www.efs-enterprises.com

Library of Congress Cataloging-in-Publication Data

Jenkins, Zeretha, 1959-
  Walking by faith : an Afro-American trilogy : a dramatic trilogy celebrating Afro-American accomplishments / by Zeretha Jenkins.-- Rev. ed.
      p. cm.
  Includes bibliographical references.
  ISBN 0-9701344-0-1 (pbk. : alk. paper)
  1. African Americans--Drama. I. Jenkins, Zeretha, 1959- Trial of the race.
II. Jenkins, Zeretha, 1959- Conversations with history. III. Jenkins, Zeretha, 1959- Afro-Americans--our pride is showing! IV. Title.
  PS3610.E547W35 2005
  812'.6--dc22
                              2005019770

First Printing

Dedication

To my beloved Mother – may God bless her soul – and my Father -- how do I find the words to say *Thank you* for giving birth to me, thus giving me this opportunity to write this book and express myself creatively. I thank you from the depths of my heart.

And to my sisters – Freda, Debra, and Vanessa – whom I cherish, *thank you* for your love and support down through the years.

To my other relatives – nieces, nephews, cousins, aunts, uncles, grandparents (whose love and support I feel all the way from Heaven), my extended family, friends, and supporters – please know that I treasure you and the faith you've had in me and my talents.

I sincerely thank *all* of you for being a *very precious* part of my life. You're *special,* indeed!

Sincere Love Forever,

Zeretha

Foreword

On the very day that I received Zeretha Jenkins' dramatic trilogy in the mail, I had in hand a newspaper article reporting the wonders of DNA and how it may link us to our history. It seems that by simply swabbing the insides of our mouth and taking a DNA sample, molecular biologists will soon be able to determine exactly where in Africa our ancestors came from before they were enslaved.

The article went on to say that knowing our origins would help "restore the specifics of identity that were deliberately damaged by slaveholders in order to make enslaved Africans seem less human."

For once I welcomed the news about DNA and its test tube ramifications, for not knowing who I am or where I came from often has me gazing at the faces and map of the motherland, feeling rootless, silently pleading: is this my tribe, my distant cousins, the place of my ancestors' birth? And as I put down the newspaper and began reading through "Walking by Faith: An Afro-American Trilogy," I soon felt like shouting, for her news was as equally exhilarating.

In this trilogy Ms. Jenkins celebrates our accomplishments in this country after our long and tortuous Middle Passage from Africa to the Americas. And in doing so, the three plays provide another view of our fractured history, beginning with the horrid days of slavery and journeying to the new millennium.

Sister Jenkins is an imaginative playwright, and using this trilogy like a swab of DNA, she connects us to our past, highlights the present, and hopes for the future. Her characters are inventive but for real: Freedom fighters Frederick Douglass and Harriet Tubman; the great historian, Dr. Carter G. Woodson; the spirited runner, Wilma Rudolph; the incomparable politician, Adam Clayton Powell Jr.; the fallen astronaut, Ronald McNair, are all here.

But there is levity here, too, for we are a people of abiding faith, given more to hope than despair. So I smile in one of the plays, "Trial of the Race," Ms. Jenkins throws in extraterrestrial beings to confront two professional sisters – circa 2000 – and then stumps me with a black history game show in "Our Pride is Showing."

"Walking by Faith: An Afro-American Trilogy" is funny, witty, graceful, scholarly, poignant. It is us; stamped with our inimitable will to survive. Thank you, Zeretha Jenkins.

– Joyce White, *Soul Food: Recipes and Reflections from African-American Churches*

Preface

WALKING BY FAITH: AN AFRO-AMERICAN TRILOGY is a dramatic collection that celebrates the Afro-American experience in America with a unique mixture of colorful characters, including lawyers, doctors, and even the extraterrestrial! Throughout its series of unexpected twists and turns, it sends a profound message that one's history and present are invaluable gems, which pave the way to one's future and ultimate survival.

TRIAL OF THE RACE

The first in the trilogy focuses on two friends – JACKIE, a very prominent judge, and DELORES, a renowned physician -- who are unexpectedly swept into another world via an alien abduction! ***TRIAL OF THE RACE*** becomes the trial of sheer survival for Jackie, Delores, and the entire race!

CONVERSATIONS WITH HISTORY

High school juniors, ALEXIS and ANDREW -- are hurled dead-smack into the eye of the hurricane when Alexis encounters a showdown with her teacher, MS. LINDEN, in what proves to be the lesson of their lives.

AFRO-AMERICANS: OUR PRIDE IS SHOWING GAME SHOW

A delightful mix of educational enhancement and fun! Presented in the format of a game show, it's an interactive piece that's sure to delight!

CONTENTS

TRIAL OF THE RACE..................................16
    SCENE 1..................................18
    SCENE 2..................................23
    SCENE 3..................................31

CONVERSATIONS WITH HISTORY..............42
    SCENE 1..................................44
    SCENE 2..................................52

AFRO-AMERICANS:
OUR PRIDE IS SHOWING!!!..............63

APPENDIX A: Preliminary Round List of Questions
(Athletes/Politicians/Civil Rights Activists & More).........78

APPENDIX B: Preliminary Round List of Questions
(Great Afro-American Heroines)..............................81

APPENDIX C: Preliminary Round List of Questions
(Entertainers & Writers)....................................83

APPENDIX D: Grand Prize Questions List....................86

ABOUT THE AUTHOR..93

TRIAL OF THE RACE

TRIAL OF THE RACE

CHARACTERS

JACKIE FONTAINE:
Judge, mid to late 40s (may be older)

DELORES (DEE) FLETCHER, M.D.:
Prominent physician, mid to late 40s (may be older)

ALIEN NO. 1:
Extraterrestrial being, age is insignificant

ALIEN NO. 2:
Extraterrestrial being, age is insignificant

HARRIET TUBMAN:
Civil Rights Leader known as the Conductor of the Underground Railroad

DR. RONALD MCNAIR:
Astronaut from the Challenger Space Shuttle

BARBARA JORDAN:
Eloquent outspoken Congresswoman from Texas

FREDERICK DOUGLASS:
Civil Rights Leader who fought to abolish slavery

MARY MCLEOD BETHUNE:
Outstanding educator and leader who established Bethune-Cookman College

18 Walking By Faith: An Afro-American Trilogy

Scene 1

SETTING: Present. Small rural town. Shopping mall parking lot. Evening. Two friends, JACKIE and DELORES (DEE), have just left the mall and are walking toward JACKIE'S car on the parking lot. JACKIE is fumbling with her purse as she searches her coat pockets then her purse for her keys.

JACKIE: Well, one thing's for sure. We don't have to search for the car this time, do we?

(Both laugh)

DEE: No m'am. Especially since it's the last one left on the lot.

JACKIE: Oh hush, Dee. You know this is all your fault.
(Still digging for keys in her purse.)

DEE: Excuse me! But did I force you to be out shopping till you dropped -- window-shopping, that is -- till closing time?

JACKIE: (Jokingly) No, no. I have no recollection of this situation being like that.

DEE: Oh, well, I guess it was all my imagination that we were the last customers to leave the mall.

JACKIE: (Playfully sarcastic) Oh, I can't say 'cause I didn't conduct a thorough search of the mall before leaving in order to conclude that we were, in fact, the actual last parties to leave the premises.

DEE: Oh my goodness, Counselor. You can skip the mumbo-jumbo legal logic. We're not in the courtroom, you know.

JACKIE: (Chuckles) I knew you'd concede. And look at that! (Pulls keys from purse) You see, I can find things rather quickly in this suitcase -- when I want -- (Pats her purse)

(Lights on the parking lot blink several times as JACKIE and DEE gasp. The lights come back on briefly. They look at each other then abruptly all lights go out again. Suddenly there's a bright light in the sky that is slowly lowering to the ground. The women are terrified.)

DEE: J-J-Jackie. D-D-Do you see what I see? (Pause as JACKIE doesn't answer.)

DEE (cont'd.): (Terrified) Jackie! Jackie?! Are you still here?

JACKIE: The way your fingernails are digging into my arms, do you think I could escape?

DEE: Ooh, I'm so glad! What is that?

JACKIE:	I don't know.

DEE:	We've got to get away. We've got to run!

JACKIE:	You're right. On the count of three, let's run for our lives.

DEE:	O.K.

JACKIE:	One ... two ... three --- (JACKIE starts to run, but DEE remains frozen in her tracks.) Dee! (As she's jerked back due to Dee's death hold on her arm) What are you doing? Would you come on!

DEE:	I-I can't ... (Panicking) I can't -- Jackie, I can't move my feet.

(JACKIE tries frantically to help DEE move but to no avail. Than DEE gasps as she notices the huge light in front of them has settled on the ground. The light is so bright that they can hardly see.)

DEE:	Jackie ... Look!!! (Points to bright light and the images of two beings* approaching them.) Mercy, Jackie. What is that?

JACKIE:	Lord, I don't know!

(Both women are terrified and begin to slowly back up.)

DEE:	What is it, J-Jackie?

(A green and a red light flash simultaneously about the stage in the direction of JACKIE and DEE, who become mesmerized with fear. The two beings look at each other and begin to slowly approach the women.)

*Refers to alien beings, which may be petite and thin with oversized heads. However, for casting purposes, the actors need not be thin or necessarily petite. Their faces, however, should be made up to resemble the stereotypical "alien" look -- i.e., large, sort of triangular-shaped head (wide at the top and narrow near its base) with huge, black, oval-shaped eyes.

DEE
(cont'd.):   Oh, my God! Jackie, what is this?

JACKIE: Aliens -- (Hesitates)

DEE: Aliens? Oh, God, I don't want to die! Come on, Jackie. Let's go!

(DEE attempts to run as does JACKIE.)

JACKIE: I can't move.

DEE: Neither can I! (Starts crying as JACKIE caresses her) We're gonna die. I just know it. We're –

JACKIE: Don't say th ---

(Aliens shine bright red light on the women. They scream then collapse as the aliens look at one another. Lights go out abruptly.)

END OF SCENE 1.

Scene 2

SETTING: Minutes later. Stage is blackened except for spotlight on JACKIE and DEE, who sit next to each other about a foot or two apart. They're coming out of their state of unconsciousness and are momentarily incoherent. Their hands are at their sides and though they appear relaxed, are not able to get up and move about. Light begins to blink.

DEE: Jackie ... Jackie ... where are we?

JACKIE: D-Dee? Dee? (Looks about in disoriented fashion) Dee, wh-where's the car? We've got to go -

DEE: Go where? I don't even know where we --

(Lights go out momentarily. Both women gasp. A deep humming sound can be heard. It soon stops. When the white spotlight comes back up, the two ALIENS can be seen standing STAGE LEFT just outside the perimeter of the light. JACKIE spots them first.)

JACKIE: Dee -- LOOK!

(DEE slowly turns her head to the left and screams as she spots the ALIENS.)

DEE: Oh, God -- ALIENS! Run!

(Both women try in vain to get up and run as the ALIENS approach and stand on the edge of the light. They stare briefly at the women then at each other. The ALIENS raise their left arms and push their wide waistbands simultaneously.)

ALIEN #1: (Monotone, very calm voice) Silence.

(Both women become silent instantly although they continue to form words with their mouths yet are unable to actually speak. They eventually desert this effort, too.)

ALIEN #1: (To JACKIE and DEE) Earthlings of the imperfect race ...

ALIEN #2: Moors.

(JACKIE and DEE, highly offended, try to defend themselves but are still mute. The ALIENS look at one another and nod. ALIEN #1 touches a series of buttons on his left wristband, which restores speech to the women.)

ALIEN #1: Speak.

JACKIE: Wh ... Wh... (Looks at DEE)

DEE: (To ALIENS) Where are we?

JACKIE: And what did you just say about us?

ALIEN #2: (To ALIEN #1 in undertone) Feisty ... And very emotional.

ALIEN #1:	(To ALIEN #2 in undertone) This is typical of this breed. Their emotions exceed their intelligence.
DEE:	(To JACKIE) Wait a minute. What did they just say?
JACKIE:	(To ALIENS) Look, you big-eyed pale so-and-so's.
DEE:	Tell'em, girl.
JACKIE:	If by chance, your comments were intended to refer to Afro-Americans, you've been highly misinformed.
ALIEN #2:	You are underachievers ... do not ascribe to the principle of a work ethic...your male counterpart is for the most part, incarcerated ... you've engaged repeatedly in immorally over-populating the Earth... and finally at the core of your limited intelligence is an insurmountable defect of inferior genes.
JACKIE: DEE:	(Simultaneously) What??!!!
JACKIE:	Look, I don't know who the --
DEE:	(Calmly) Jackie --
JACKIE:	(Pauses and regains her composure) Thank you, girl. (To ALIENS) As I was saying, I don't know who you are or what your intentions might be, but --

(ALIENS glance at each other.)

JACKIE (cont'd.): But you don't know the first thing about Afro-American Earthlings to use your terminology.

DEE: Tell'em, girlfriend!

JACKIE: For your information, these two women (Points to herself and DEE) of African ancestry of alleged 'limited intelligence happen to be Delores K. Fletcher - M.D. --

(DEE nods in acknowledgement.)

JACKIE (cont'd.): -- and the --

DEE: The Honorable Judge Jacqueline T. Fontaine!

JACKIE: (Nods appreciatively) Why thank you, Dee. The ALIENS stare at each other in amazement.)

ALIEN #1: There are -- as you Earthlings say -- exceptions -- to every rule.

DEE: (To ALIENS) You know, you two "swell-heads" remind me of a group of people on Earth we refer to as racists.

ALIEN #1: That is impossible. Our intelligence is superior to that of even the brightest Earthling. Therefore, no such comparison exists.

JACKIE: I object to that!

ALIEN #1: You can object to nothing—

JACKIE: Oh, yes I can -- as long as I have God as my Guide, truth as my shield, and the history of my people to firmly stand upon. Yes I can.

(The ALIENS move into the darkness and talk among themselves before returning to the edge of the light.)

ALIEN #1: (Sarcastically) Very well, Judge. Then the burden of proof for your whole race rests on your shoulders.

JACKIE: What?

DEE: What are you talking about? You're the ones who are supposed to be of "superior" intelligence. You should already know of the accomplishments of our race.

ALIEN #2: The fact is no such record of these alleged accomplishments exists.

DEE: I'm not surprised, especially according to statistics, even you Aliens discriminate! I mean, for the most part, you sure don't go out of your way abducting minorities, now do you?

JACKIE: (Snickers then in undertone to DEE)
Talk about universal discrimination!

(Both women chuckle)

ALIEN #2: (Sternly to DEE) If these "accomplishments" exist, prove it.

ALIEN #1: If you do not, you -- being our final two Earthly abductees will have the distinct honor of initiating our plans to immediately remove your kind from the face of your planet.

JACKIE: DEE:
      (Simultaneously)
What?   Huh?

JACKIE: Are you crazy?

ALIEN #2: Quite the contrary. We have studied your planet, and its human forms for the equivalent of centuries, according to your Earth time. Your people have proven inferior.

ALIEN #1: We will give you a final chance to prove your worthiness. (Touches his right wrist band) You are free to use any intelligent means of defense.

DEE: Does that include resurrecting the dead?

JACKIE: (In undertone) Dee, what are you talking about?

(The ALIENS consult between themselves.)

ALIEN #1: To reiterate the fact of our superior intelligence --

(JACKIE and DEE sigh loudly and shake their heads in disgust)

ALIEN #1
(cont'd.): --death is but a state of mind among members of the human race. However, in our world, it does not exist.

(JACKIE and DEE look at each other puzzled.)

ALIEN #1
(cont'd.): Should you wish to summon such witnesses on behalf of your defense, consider it done. (Touches several buttons on his right wristband and green lights "dance" about the stage. DEE and JACKIE are frightened.)

ALIEN #2: There's no need to be afraid.

ALIEN #1: But remember ... you can call only 5 witnesses, and your have 10 Earth minutes to present your entire defense.

JACKIE: Ten minutes?

DEE: How do you expect us to --

ALIEN #1: You're wasting time. Good luck -- whatever that means -- and --

(ALIENS begin descending into the darkness.)

JACKIE: Hey, wait a minute. How do you do this? You haven't told us how to actually summon our witnesses -- from the dead.

ALIEN #1: Simply call them. Now rise and begin.

(ALIENS continue backing into the darkness until they're off stage. Immediately the green lights cease and are replaced by a red beam that will act as a sort of Transport Chamber for the deceased witnesses who will be called to testify.
The stage then FADES TO BLACK.)

END OF SCENE 2.

Scene 3

SETTING: JACKIE and DEE are up and about and going over their list of witnesses.

DEE: Well, Counselor... I mean, Judge ... here's our list of witness. (Hands JACKIE the list) Do your best. We have too much riding on this verdict. Give it your best shot.

(JACKIE nods and takes the list.)

DEE (cont'd.): And remember, girl. No matter how things turn out, I'll always love you. (Hugs JACKIE while fighting back tears)

JACKIE: I love you, too. (Begins to cry)

ALIEN #1 (OFFSTAGE): You have 9 minutes.

DEE: (Wipes tears from JACKIE'S face) Go 'head, girl. Giv'em -- you know what!

(Both women chuckle.)

JACKIE: Well, since there isn't any time for opening statements, I'll get right down to business. I'd like to call as my first witness none other than our great

JACKIE
(cont'd.):   heroine -- the *Underground Conductress,* Harriet Ross Tubman!

HARRIET TUBMAN:
(Boldly steps into the spotlight then speaks with authority) I am the woman they call Moses. At times I've even been called General Tubman. Born a slave in Dorchester County, Maryland, I overcame my oppression and freed myself at age 13 of the cruel bondage that was heaped on my people. But that was not enough for me. No sir. I made up my mind that no matter what the consequences, I would do all in my power to set my people free. And that's why I became a Conductor. That's right ... of the Underground Railroad -- the only such *freedom train* of its day. In my lifetime I transported over 300 women, men, and children to freedom. And I never lost a passenger. And you have the nerve to think Black folks don't mount to nothing? Well, (Sarcastically) *gentlemen*, it gives me great pleasure to say that you and anybody else that dares think such dumb things as that must be a fool and nothing less. Now go and analyze that!

(HARRIET turns and fades into the darkness.)

ALIEN #1:	ALIEN #2:
	(Simultaneously) Humph! The nerve!

ALIEN #1:   (Annoyed) Let's get on with this. Call your next witness.

JACKIE: I present to you laser physicist -- Dr. Ronald McNair.

(DR. MCNAIR steps into the spotlight. He's dressed in his astronaut uniform.)

DR. RONALD MCNAIR:
Gentlemen ... Our paths have no doubt crossed -- in orbit, that is.

(Light flickers momentarily as we hear the mumblings of the ALIENS as they react to MCNAIR'S statement. Light then returns to full beam.)

ALIEN #1: Continue.

DR. RONALD MCNAIR:
As an astronaut on board the Challenger space shuttle, in 1984, I was the first to actually execute a runway landing of that shuttle at none other than Kennedy Space Center. This was just one of the firsts I accomplished during my lifetime. On my final Challenger mission, I was responsible for a satellite known as the Spartan-Halley, which was intended to actually track, or monitor, the orbit of -- you guessed it -- Halley's comet. And talking about firsts, put this one in the record books. I was the first ever to give a jazz concert in space to my fellow astronauts. And like Charlie *the Bird* Parker, my saxophone and I were in "Jazz Heaven". Now tell me (Snaps fingers) I'm not a heavy brother! (Jubilantly) Well, all right then!

(Spotlight fades. MCNAIR exits.)

JACKIE: Now I'd like to introduce you to one of the most outstanding politicians and greatest speakers of all time -- the Texas attorney – Barbara Jordan.

(We hear BARBARA JORDAN'S footsteps on the blackened stage. Then abruptly the spotlight comes up but not immediately on JORDAN.)

BARBARA JORDAN:
(To the spotlight very serenely) Thank you... I'm over here.

(The spotlight then quickly focuses on MS. JORDAN, who takes a deep breath and then slowly and deliberately exhales majestically as she looks from one corner of the room to the other.)

BARBARA JORDAN:
I have never been one to *bite* my tongue, or run from a good fight. My record as a tough Congresswoman attests to that fact. And certainly I have no plans to change any time soon -- or EVER -- for that matter. People frequently think of me as the tough-talking Texan who can back up what she says. And it was that spirit plus my religious roots -- Baptist, I might add -- that propelled me forward into public office as the first Afro-American female from a Southern state to be elected into the U.S. Congress. And if you think that was an easy feat -- especially in 1966 -- then

BARBARA JORDAN (cont'd.):
think again. When I graduated - ah, magna cum laude -- from Texas Southern University, I was well aware of the massive ignorance that was still rampart in America when it came to the topic of my people. But I can stand here today and honestly state that your inexcusable blissful ignorance regarding the extreme intelligence of the Afro-American people is, without doubt, an utter travesty of your alleged extra-terrestrial *intellect*.

ALIEN #1: (Infuriated, addresses JACKIE) Call your next witness.

(Spotlight disappears abruptly and rudely from MS. JORDAN.)

BARBARA JORDAN'S VOICE:
(Cool, calm, collected and courteous as she addresses the ALIENS) Likewise -- good evening to you, too -- (Sarcastically) *gentlemen*.

(We hear MS. JORDAN'S slow stately footsteps as she leaves the stage. They are, indeed, indicative of her refusal to be rushed or brushed aside.)

JACKIE: Thank you, Attorney Jordan. My next witness is none other than the irrepressible abolitionist, orator, and writer – Frederick Douglass.

FREDERICK DOUGLASS:
Born as a slave, I never let that hold me back from getting my education and fighting to abolish injustices, especially those imposed on my people. After educating myself, I used my skills and determination to speak out against those who so casually imposed the disgraceful and immoral injustice of slavery. I boldly declared to all willing and able to hear that I am for any movement whenever there is a good cause to promote, a right to assert, a chain to be broken, a burden to be removed, or a wrong to be redressed. I believe in freedom for all...in the rights of women ... in education for every citizen of this country and throughout the world. I firmly believe in the reform of our penal system. And I do strongly believe in universal peace. I must say with a heavy heart, indeed, that the struggles, which I have endured for human equality, have yet to be resolved. In this day and age, we must be alert to the fact that although the faces of the players in this game of life have changed, don't be deceived -- for the game, indeed, is still the same.

(Spotlight fades quickly from MR. DOUGLASS, plunging him into darkness. He exits.)

ALIEN #2: (To JACKIE and DEE) You have 2 minutes.

DEE: (Whispering to JACKIE) Boy, they're real jerks, aren't they?

JACKIE: (Whispering) And that's putting it very nicely. (To ALIENS) Gentlemen... I present to you the indomitable civil rights activist, educator, and leader – *MS. MARY MCLEOD BETHUNE.*

Spotlight up on the majestic MARY MCLEOD BETHUNE, who stands proudly at CENTER STAGE.)

MARY MCLEOD BETHUNE:
(Grandly and eloquently) It is truly an honor to be invited here for this most unusual of occasions. As a very determined Afro-American woman who waded through one of the most oppressive eras of this country's history, I never, and I repeat never, gave up the faith. Yes, I was very blessed to have received a formal education, which not only paved the way for my personal achievements, but which allowed me to serve my people in their endless quest for equality and justice. As a people, we must unite and be willing to serve one another in order to forge ahead collectively as a people. I served diligently all of my life in various capacities in order that this cause might come into fruition. I reigned for numerous years as the President, Director, and even in some cases, as Founder of such worthy organizations as: 1) the National Association of Colored Women; 2) the National Council of Negro Women; 3) the Association for the Study of Negro Life and History; and 4) the National Youth Administration's Division of Negro

MARY MCLEOD BETHUNE (cont'd.):
    Affairs. I also served proudly as a member of Franklin Delano Roosevelt's Federal Council of Negro Affairs. It is my firm belief that no human being should walk the face of this earth and then dare die without leaving a legacy on which future generations can build upon, profit from and farther advance themselves in preparation for the legacy they should some day leave for others. This is why I established Bethune-Cookman College in Florida -- so that my people could actually reap the fruits of my legacy. It is fact that faith coupled with hard work can yield miracles. (Pauses then turns to and addresses JACKIE and DEE) Jacqueline and Delores -- always remember that your diligent efforts to save our race are not in vain. I thank you for your diligent efforts. (Begins backing out of the beam of light and into the darkness) God bless you both. (Exits)

(The Spotlight flickers and the beam narrows as JACKIE and DEE look at each other in fear. They caress each other.)

JACKIE: DEE:
    (Simultaneously as they begin to cry)
        No matter what -- I love you, girl. I love you, Dee!
        I love you!

(Spotlight abruptly fades to black and remains out for a few seconds as we hear an intense low-pitched humming sound. Then there's dead silence. A dim light comes up. Both women are at

CENTER STAGE while JACKIE is still frantically searching her purse for her keys. DEE has her hand on her hip while patting her foot on the pavement as she impatiently waits. They are in the identical playful mood that they were in prior to their abduction.)

DEE: (Sarcastically) Oh, anytime before the end of the next century! Girl, you haven't found those keys yet?

JACKIE: (Sarcastically) Uh, uh, uh. Patience is a virtue, isn't it!

DEE: Well?

JACKIE: Oh, but of course, I've found them. (Still searching then sarcastically) But I just happen to love keeping you in suspense!

(DEE gives a quick sarcastic smile)

DEE: (Looking at watch) Well, look, *Madame Prankster*, if you don't -- (Does a double take in looking at her watch) What? It's one o'clock in the morning, Jackie! I can't believe this!

JACKIE: (As she gleefully pulls her keys out of her purse and then dangles them in the air) Oh, hush girl. Come on. We're in business!

(Both women begin approaching the exit at STAGE LEFT as JACKIE leads the way to her car, which is never visible on stage. They're laughing and joking as the spotlight begins to fade.)

DEE: Girl, it's so late, we might as well go get breakfast!

JACKIE: Breakfast? I thought you were trying to lose weight!

DEE: Oh, uh-uh. That was last year!

JACKIE: What?

DEE: Besides – there's no need to improve upon perfection!

(They exit.)

OFFSTAGE:

JACKIE: Say what? Girl, get your over-inflated ego in this car and please be quiet. My goodness!

DEE: Ah, my goodness nothing!

(Their voices diminish as they continue laughing and joking until the spotlight fades to black.)

THE END.

CONVERSATIONS WITH HISTORY

CONVERSATIONS WITH

HISTORY

CHARACTERS

ALEXIS:
High School Junior & top candidate as valedictorian

ANDREW:
High School Junior who is a good friend of Alexis

MS. LINDEN:
Alexis's English class teacher, 20s - 30s

VERONICA:
One of Alexis's classmates

DR. CARTER G. WOODSON:
Outstanding writer and historian

WILMA RUDOLPH:
Track and Field star who was an Olympic Gold Medallist

ADAM CLAYTON POWELL, JR.:
Legendary minister, Congressman, and Civil Rights Leader

MAHALIA JACKSON:
Queen of Gospel Music

Scene 1

SETTING: Present. High School. Student Government Room near the close of the school day. At CENTER STAGE is a table with many books and some notebooks on top of it. ALEXIS, the potential Junior class valedictorian, is sitting at the table with her head buried in books. Three or four other students are in the room looking at books on the shelves. ALEXIS looks distressed and troubled. She then cradles her chin between her fists while resting her elbows on the table. She stares blankly straight ahead into space. In walks from STAGE RIGHT her friend and fellow classmate, ANDREW, who nearly walks past the table before noticing her. He enters with a book and notebook under his arm. He then places them on the table then drops his smile abruptly. He slowly backs up while waving his hands above his head in an attempt to get ALEXIS'S attention. ALEXIS, however, appears to be in a trance, and still does not see him. He then leans over the right side of the table so that he's only about 3" or 4" from ALEXIS'S face.

ANDREW: (In a rather loud but playful voice) YES, ALEXIS! I'll MARRY YOU! (He then puckers his lips in a very exaggerated way as though expecting a kiss)

(ALEXIS as well as everyone else in earshot is startled. Everyone present stops doing what they're doing and turn to observe ALEXIS and ANDREW. ALEXIS is highly embarrassed and momentarily covers her face with her hands. Eventually the others return to what they were originally doing.)

ALEXIS: Andrew, what are you doing?

ANDREW: (Still leaning near her with a big smile on his face) Just trying to get a beautiful lady's attention!

ALEXIS: Well, you've definitely achieved that!

(Both laugh.)

ALEXIS: (Pointing toward chair to her right) Here, sit down.

ANDREW: Thanks. (Pulls chair back and sits) Are you all right? You look like you were lost in space or something!

ALEXIS: I don't know what I'm going to do, Andrew.

ANDREW: About what?

ALEXIS: This -- (Hands ANDREW her assignment pad that's open to her English assignment)

ANDREW: (Reads assignment silently and then appears stunned) What's this?

ALEXIS: My assignment for English class.

ANDREW: Who's the teacher?

ALEXIS: None other than *the* Ms. Eleanor Linden.

ANDREW: (With big smile on his face as he places his hand over his heart) You mean the gorgeous Perfect 10+?!

ALEXIS: (Sighs loudly then playfully glares at ANDREW) Well ... it just so happens that that gorgeous Perfect 10+ doesn't have a clue as to who she is, where she came from, or where she's going.

ANDREW: (Gets up) Now I can help her with the third one! (Stretches out his arms, starts swaying, and then romantically begins beckoning as he tries to hum or maybe even "sing" his next line) Just come on my way, Ms. Lin-DEN. Come right into my arms.

(ALEXIS glares at ANDREW and shakes her head as he continues in his fantasy world by acting as though he were slow dragging with Ms. Linden in his arms. The other students looking on are snickering at the sight of ANDREW. One girl is laughing so hard that she runs out of the room holding her mouth in an attempt to keep from laughing out aloud. ANDREW seems shocked by her reaction.)

ALEXIS: O.K., Mr. "Singing Casanova with heartburn and club feet", you want to take off the dance shoes now?

(ANDREW stops abruptly and is embarrassed as he notices the other students falling out laughing at him, too. Quickly he regains his composure, nervously clears his throat and then walks back over to the right side of the table but doesn't sit just yet.)

ALEXIS: (Very deadpan as she reaches out and touches ANDREW'S hand.) Andrew, have you had ample time to make an absolute fool of yourself? Or do you need a little more time?

(Other students burst into more laughter. ANDREW sighs loudly.)

ALEXIS (cont'd.): I'm only asking 'cause I wouldn't want to rush you -- if -- you needed more time.

ANDREW: Ha! Ha! Ha! (Pulls chair back, quickly sits then answers sarcastically) Girl, you are just too funny! Looks like you missed your calling as a comedienne.

(ALEXIS smiles widely in an attempt to keep from laughing out aloud.)

ANDREW (cont'd.): Yo ... it's like -- (Using exaggerated hand gestures) I was trying to cheer you up. And, ah, you're in tears laughing at me. Man!

ALEXIS: (Playing along with ANDREW'S game) Oh...that's what you were trying to do?!

ANDREW: (Hesitates then nervously answers) Ah... yeah? I-I mean -- yeah! That's exactly what I was doing. (Smiles slyly) But you have to admit --when you're as lovely as Ms. Linden, do you really need to know all that jazz about where you've been and where you're going?

ALEXIS: Andrew, I'm really surprised at you. Don't you see that that way of thinking is exactly the problem? Too many of us don't have an inkling as to who we really are. And what's sadder than that is that we don't seem to care either.

ANDREW: C'mon, *Lexis*. Lighten up. You too young to be this deep in this political stuff!

ALEXIS: Young? Andy, in less that two years, we'll be adults. When do you suggest we start getting serious about the world and issues that directly affect us and particularly *our* race? Huh?

ANDREW: Hey, look. All I'm saying is I don't want to get sucked into this political thang till ... till ... well, till my late 20s or even '30s. (Brief silence as ALEXIS takes a deep breath and tries to "digest" ANDREW'S last remark)

ALEXIS: (Emphatically) The point is, Andrew -- that Ms. Linden wants us to write an essay on this topic: *Focus On The Future ... Bury The Past.*

ANDREW: What?

ALEXIS: Her stance is that the past or one's history -- is a cancelled check. And, therefore, not relevant to one's future. (Chuckles in disgust) She even went so far as to say that the past should be forgotten! (Buries her face in the palms of her hands)

ANDREW: (Puts his arm around ALEXIS) All joking aside. Why would she make an assignment like that? Especially since it's Black History Month.

ALEXIS: (Looks up) Why do you think?

ANDREW: I-I don't know. I mean I thought Ms. Linden was a sister who had it together. I mean -- beauty ... (Smiles suggestively)

(ALEXIS gently pulls away from him and folds her arms briefly as she sits back in her chair.)

ANDREW (cont'd.): (Nervously) and... and brains to match! (Smiles innocently)

ALEXIS: Oh, it's true -- she's very intelligent, and I have a lot of respect for her. BUT -- somewhere down the line she seemed to have misunderstood the

ALEXIS
(cont'd.):   significance of our past and how it impacts on both our present and future.

ANDREW: But you can't tell her that. So what are you gonna do?

ALEXIS: (Pauses and takes a deep breath) I'm not gonna do the assignment. (Jumps up)

ANDREW: I know you buggin'! Girl, you the front-runner for valedictorian of this class and you gonna run the risk of blowing that just 'cause of some essay?

(ANDREW walks DOWN STAGE and continues facing audience. ALEXIS gets up, walks over to him, and touches him on the shoulder.)

ALEXIS: Andrew, I know you don't --

ANDREW: (Walks DOWN STAGE LEFT away from her) Man, this is too much! To find out my two favorite African Queens are both trippin' -- in the same day! Man, this is too much on a man's -- (Does "heart-throb" gesture in this fashion: With right hand, he pats his chest open-handed over his heart 3 times) -- heart!

ALEXIS: (Flattered, she kisses his cheek) How sweet of you!

(ANDREW does the heartthrob gesture with left hand behind ALEXIS'S back as she kisses him. She's not aware of him doing this gesture.)

ANDREW: Wow! (Nervously clears his throat) I mean, so what are you gonna do? When is the assignment due?

ALEXIS: Tomorrow.

ANDREW: Ahh -- (Sighs then hugs ALEXIS) We'll think of something. Lady --I promise we'll think up something.

LIGHTS FADE TO BLACK.

END OF SCENE 1.

Scene 2

SETTING: Next day. MS. LINDEN'S classroom. UPSTAGE CENTER is the podium, which faces the audience. On each side of the podium are about 6 – 8 desks angled diagonally toward the podium. The classroom is decorated in a typical fashion, which includes a chalkboard, globe, books of classic plays, novels, short story collections, etc. ALEXIS is sitting on the right hand side of the classroom and behind her are 4 people dressed in costumes from various eras. On the other side of classroom are 4 – 8 additional students. VERONICA, one of ALEXIS'S classmates, is at the podium giving the final part of her essay at the opening of this scene.

VERONICA: And these are my reasons why we as a race must move forward into the future -- minus the past and all "baggage" affiliated with it. Thank you.

(Gathers her papers and returns to her seat as her fellow classmates and MS. LINDEN applaud. MS. LINDEN then steps behind the podium.)

Walking By Faith: An Afro-American Trilogy

MS. LINDEN: Thank you, Veronica. That was excellent.
(Some of the students look at each other and chuckle under their breath in disagreement with MS. LINDEN'S statement.)
(Looks briefly at her watch) Well, class, we have only about 10 minutes and time for maybe one more essay. But first I'd like to -- let's see -- (Shuffles through papers on podium and finds Memorandum from the Drama Coach) Ah, yes, here it is. Class, I'd like to acknowledge our guests. (Looks in direction of 4 people dressed in costumes in back of room) Let's see, according to this memo I received from Mr. Fredricks, our Drama Coach, we'd be having some guests who'd like to do a little presentation since it's Black History Month. Please (To 4 GUESTS in costumes) -- come now with your presentation.

(The 4 GUESTS arise as does ALEXIS and come before the class. MS. LINDEN is shocked to see ALEXIS accompany the group and shows mild disapproval but says nothing.)

ALEXIS: (Behind podium)
To help do justice to this topic that we're faced with, four members of the Drama Club have decided to help me present the necessity to respect our past yet not dwell on it and certainly not bury it either.

(ALEXIS'S classmates look at one another, some smiling in agreement with ALEXIS while others are clearly uneasy and glance at MS. LINDEN, who glares briefly at ALEXIS.)

MS. LINDEN: Alexis, please move on. We have only about 10 minutes. (The students, surprised by MS. LINDEN'S abrupt interruption, glance at her uneasily.)

ALEXIS: Without further adieu -- (Steps away from the podium as the first GUEST, DR. CARTER G. WOODSON, steps up to the podium.)

DR. CARTER G. WOODSON: Fellow Sisters and Brothers, I am the definitive Dr. Carter G. Woodson, writer and historian. Never ever let anyone sever your bloodline with your past. After having received my doctoral degree in 1912 from Harvard University, I never stopped being educated and educating. My life-long goal was that of unveiling the ignorance of all people by revealing to the world numerous historical facts about our people that had been deliberately erased from the history of the United States. This is why I published my much needed and most popular book, *THE MIS-EDUCATION OF THE NEGRO*. In fact, it was my organization, the Association for the Study of Negro Life and History, which in 1926, established National Negro History Week. It's now such a blessing to see its evolution into Black History Month. I now challenge you to expand beyond that accomplishment until we achieve equal representation of our history not one month of the year but all twelve months of the year -- from this time forth. Thank you.

Walking By Faith: An Afro-American Trilogy   55

(DR. WOODSON returns to his seat as every one applauds -- even MS. LINDEN but who does so reluctantly. GUEST NO. 2 -- WILMA RUDOLPH -- approaches the podium.)

WILMA RUDOLPH:
Some call me Wilma Rudolph and have dubbed me the *World's Fastest Woman* when I won these -- (Pointing to the medals around her neck) -- three Gold Medals in the 1960 Olympics. But I must concede that that's not my greatest accomplishment. My greatest accomplishment has been perseverance. I have fought the odds all of my life. As a child I was afflicted with polio and scarlet fever and as a result, had to wear a leg brace till age 12. But my real struggles started at birth when I was born Black but proud *and* female. I believe in defying the odds even when racism would have me believe I couldn't achieve because of my color and when sexism tried to hold me back at every turn. I said boldly unloose these shackles for this Black woman is gonna make her race proud of her someday. And I did...through perseverance... through faith in God ... through knowing the struggles of my ancestors and knowing that they, too, persevered. Yes some call me Wilma and that's just fine. But Perseverance has a nice ring to it, too.

(EVERYONE applauds. MS. RUDOLPH returns to her seat as the flamboyant ADAM CLAYTON POWELL, JR., approaches the podium.)

ADAM CLAYTON POWELL, JR.:
I don't need an introduction, but (Sarcastically with a chuckle) who am I to *break* from tradition?

(EVERYONE laughs.)

ADAM CLAYTON POWELL, JR. (cont'd.):
I am the daring, the indomitable ADAM CLAYTON POWELL, JR. Oh, I know you know all about my legacy as a minister, Congressman, and Civil Rights Activist. But I want to talk to you not about my career but about that one word that preceded my titles. And that precious word is *legacy*. You see, a legacy is, indeed, a priceless gift. More precious than the rarest of stones. It is that something – those accomplishments -- those stepping stones to the future that pave a solid foundation beneath your feet that enable you, your generation, and generations to follow, the means -- the road map -- by which the next generation can gain knowledge and strength. A legacy enables future generations to weather the storms which lie ahead. And *our* legacies represent the preparatory stage for our race's future. For without them, we know not from whence we came. We know not who we are. And we most definitely do not know where we are going. Let it go on record -- *this day* -- that I firmly believe that if you leave the face of this earth without leaving behind a *legacy* for your future brothers and sisters, you have without doubt, failed your race. *Keep the faith, baby. Keep the faith.*

(EVERYONE, except MS. LINDEN, stands and applauds as they cheer. ADAM CLAYTON POWELL, JR. returns to his seat. The fourth and final GUEST -- MAHALIA JACKSON, very spiritually approaches the podium.)

MAHALIA JACKSON:
    (As she approaches the podium) Hallelujah! Hallelujah! Praise God in Heaven! (Behind the podium) Woo -- hallelujah! I feel like having church after that message, Rev. Powell.

(ADAM CLAYTON POWELL, JR. acknowledges MAHALIA'S compliment by nodding his head and waving his hand.)

MAHALIA JACKSON (cont'd.):
    Thank you, Jesus.

(MAHALIA then breaks out on one of her songs. SUGGESTED SONG: *SURE DO NEED HIM NOW*. MAHALIA sings a verse or two, accompanied by all present, who sing the chorus. MS. LINDEN doesn't sing, but she claps her hands and has been touched by the Holy Spirit and enlightened. The singing dies down in the background, but the music continues as MAHALIA speaks.)

MAHALIA JACKSON (cont'd.):
    Young people, I'm here to tell you today that it doesn't matter *how* connected you are to your past, your present, or your future if *God* isn't in the picture. In other words, all your work will be in vain. These are critical times you're living in. And although a lot of us are going around here referring

MAHALIA JACKSON (cont'd.):
> to each other as brothers and sisters, it doesn't mean a thing if God is not the Head of your life. Put Him first, and you can achieve any goals and overcome any obstacles that might try to block your path. But when troubles try to get you down, don't give up. You've got to have the faith to *MOVE ON UP A LITTLE HIGHER*!

(Some of the students shout for joy while others continue singing *SURE DO NEED HIM NOW*.)

MAHALIA JACKSON (cont'd.):
> Despite the obstacles that block your path ... despite enemies on every side ... MOVE ---

EVERYONE:
> (Responding in call and answer fashion as a congregation 'answers' or responds to a minister during a sermon) Move!

MAHALIA JACKSON (cont'd.):
> -- ON UP A LITTLE HIGHER ... when the forces of evil taunt you, harass you...when racism says you are nothing and cannot achieve.... **MOVE** --

CROWD:
> -- *ON UP A LITTLE HIGHER!* And some day when you've reached the Promised Land, you'll look back -- Hallelujah! -- and wonder ... and wonder ... Lord, *HOW I GOT OVER*!

(CROWD cheers again)

MAHALIA JACKSON:
> *GOD + FAITH + PERSEVERENCE =*
> *WE SHALL OVERCOME!*

(CROWD erupts in cheers as MAHALIA leaves the podium and heads toward the back of the room. The cheering and singing swell as everyone is caught up in the moment. They don't notice MAHALIA and the others as they quietly depart via the rear of the classroom DOWNSTAGE RIGHT.
MS. LINDEN then approaches the podium.)

MS. LINDEN: (Looking about the classroom for the 4 GUESTS) We'd like to thank the members of the Drama Department for their fabulous performances.

(EVERYBODY applauds and begins looking about the room for the 4 assumed actors.)

MS. LINDEN (cont'd.):
I can't get over their likenesses to the actual heroes and heroines they portrayed. I sure would like to meet their make-up artist. (Still looking about for the GUESTS) Let's see -- I don't see them. Well, perhaps they had to leave and --

(ANDREW bursts into the classroom from DOWNSTAGE RIGHT. He's panting and out of breath.)

ANDREW: Alexis! ... Alexis!

(ALEXIS, startled, jumps out of her seat and goes DOWNSTAGE CENTER to check on him. The others, including MS. LINDEN, who's annoyed by the interruption, look on, startled, too, at first.)

ALEXIS: Andrew, what's the matter?

ANDREW: (Still winded) Alexis... I--I'm sorry.

ALEXIS: About what?

ANDREW: Y--Your essay. I wanted to help you out so you wouldn't get an 'F'.

ALEXIS: But you did.

ANDREW: No. I wanted to though. I was gonna get some friends from the Drama Department to come and do a skit or some recitations on behalf of Black History Month, but they're out of town ... participating in a Drama Festival.

ALEXIS: (Baffled) But they did.

ANDREW: What?

ALEXIS: Four of them. And the amazing thing is that they were dead ringers for Mahalia Jackson, Adam Clayton Powell, Jr., Wilma Rudolph, and Dr. Carter G. Woodson.

ANDREW: (Stunned) But who were they?

ALEXIS: (In disbelief) Come on, Andrew. You didn't send them?

ANDREW: No. (Pause) So who were they?

(ALEXIS and ANDREW look at each other in bewilderment as MS. LINDEN approaches and stares at ANDREW.)

ALEXIS: Angels!

ANDREW: (As MS. LINDEN puts her hand on ANDREW'S shoulder) Oh, Ms. Linden --

ALEXIS: Ms. Linden, this is my friend, Andrew.

MS. LINDEN: Yes, I've seen him around school a time or two. How do you do, Andrew?

ANDREW: (Nervously) F-Fine -- I-I mean, pleased to meet you -- (As an aside as he smiles widely) -- *finally!* (Very apologetically in full voice) I'm sorry I interrupted your class.

MS. LINDEN: All is forgiven. (Turns to ALEXIS) But...if you put me on the spot again like you did today, young lady, you're going to be in very hot water! Understand?

ALEXIS: I'm sorry, Ms. Linden. It won't happen again.

MS. LINDEN: All is forgiven.

(MS. LINDEN and ALEXIS hug as ANDREW looks on longingly.)

ANDREW: (To MS. LINDEN) Could I have one of those, too?

MS. LINDEN: Sure, Andrew. Why not?

(MS. LINDEN hugs ANDREW, who then does his signature "heart-throb" gesture, but this time, he also raises one of his legs and gently shakes it, thus, signifying how "electrifyingly' wonderful the hug is. ALEXIS, smiling, looks on and shakes her head in response to ANDREW'S gesture.)

ANDREW: Wow!

(He pauses then folds his arms in the same way and tradition signified by the marchers in the Civil Rights Movement. He then takes Ms. LINDEN'S hand and bursts joyously and unexpectedly into the chorus of a song. SUGGESTED SONG: *WE SHALL OVERCOME*).

ANDREW: (Singing *WE SHALL OVERCOME - Chorus*).

(Ms. LINDEN and ALEXIS, both shocked by the sudden and slightly off-key singing of ANDREW, smile and join in as they, too, fold their arms and hold hands in the traditional way as the Civil Rights activists of the 1960's. The other students stand, fold their arms, hold hands and join in, too. The audience should stand and join in, too, as several verses and choruses are sung.

(THE LIGHTS FADE TO BLACK as the last chorus is sung.)

THE END.

AFRO-AMERICANS:

OUR PRIDE

IS SHOWING!!!

GAME SHOW

AFRO-AMERICANS: OUR PRIDE IS SHOWING!!! GAME SHOW

CHARACTERS

TV GAME SHOW HOST/HOSTESS:
Male or female, young to middle-aged

PRODUCTION ASSISTANT:
Male or female, any age

PANELIST NO. 1:
Game Show Famous Facts Panelist

PANELIST No. 2:
Game Show Famous Facts Panelist

PANELIST No. 3:
Game Show Famous Facts Panelist

ASSISTANT:
Game Show Host/Hostess's Helper

SHOW CONTESTANTS: CONTESTANT NO. 1
                            CONTESTANT NO. 2
                            CONTESTANT NO. 3
Adults/Young Adults - Members of the audience

SETTING: Present. TV studio for the game show, ***AFRO-AMERICANS – OUR PRIDE IS SHOWING.*** The Hose/Hostess is standing DOWNSTAGE CENTER; the three PANELISTS – each representing a different category of questions relating to Afro-Americans – are sitting behind a desk, which is DOWNSTAGE LEFT. The categories are:

1) Athletes/Politicians/Civil Rights Activists & More;

2) Great Afro-American Heroines;

3) Entertainers & Writers.

At DOWNSTAGE RIGHT is the desk behind which each of the 3 CONTESTANTS will sit or stand.

AT RISE: LIGHTS come up and we see a PRODUCTION ASSISTANT extremely DOWNSTAGE LEFT near the wings.

PRODUCTION ASSISTANT:

> (To HOST/HOSTESS as he/she counts down verbally while using fingers on one hand to correspond to the countdown)
> Five ... Four ... Three ... Two ... One --
> (Signals to let HOST/HOSTESS know he/she's *ON THE AIR*)

HOST/HOSTESS:

> (To AUDIENCE) Good morning/afternoon/evening, Ladies and Gentlemen. Welcome to our first annual *AFRO-AMERICANS: OUR PRIDE IS SHOWING GAME SHOW!* We are being televised live and, therefore, would like to say a BIG THANK YOU to our studio audience for your participation and support.
> (Claps as he/she acknowledges the AUDIENCE)
> Thank you. And now without further adieu, I'd like to introduce the members of

HOST/HOSTESS (cont'd.):

> our FAMOUS FACTS PANEL. Please meet PANELIST NO. 1 (Pointing to PANELIST NO. 1) -- (INTRODUCE PANELIST). Thank you. And please meet -- (Pointing to PANELIST NO.2) -- PANELIST NO. 2 -- (INTRODUCE PANELIST 2). And last but not least, please welcome PANELIST NO. 3 -- (Pointing to PANELIST NO.3) -- (INTRODUCE PANELIST).
> (To PANELISTS) Thank you, Panelists.
> (To AUDIENCE) And now I'd like to briefly explain the rules of our game so we can get this show on the road. First, we're going to select 3 contestants from the audience. We will select a number and give each of the contestants a chance to guess that number. Whoever guesses closest to the number without going over the number will start the game by selecting 1 of 3 categories from which the first question will be asked. You will each have an equal chance to answer the question correctly. Whenever you think you know the answer to a question, ring your buzzer/bell. The first to sound

HOST/HOSTESS (cont'd.):
> his or her buzzer/bell will be given the first chance to answer the question. Whoever sounds his/her buzzer/bell first will have 5 seconds to correctly answer the question. If you answer it correctly, then you get to choose the category of the next question you'd like to answer. If you get that right, you keep going until you give the wrong answer. If that should happen, then your opponent to your immediate right then gets the opportunity to pick the next category of the next question. Again, whoever sounds his/her buzzer/bell first, gets the first crack at the question. If you get it right, you keep going until you miss. Then we just repeat the whole process all over again. At the end of our PRELIMINARY ROUND, whatever 2 contestants with the highest scores advance to the GRAND PRIZE ROUND. The GRAND PRIZE QUESTION, which is worth *1,000* points, will be asked. Whoever sounds his/her buzzer/bell first, gets the first shot at the question. If that person answers correctly, he/she is our GRAND PRIZE

HOST/HOSTESS (cont'd.):

WINNER. If the contestant answers incorrectly, however, then the other contestant has a chance to answer it correctly. If he/she does, then that contestant becomes our GRAND PRIZE WINNER. If, by chance neither answers the question correctly, then we proceed to the next GRAND PRIZE QUESTION. The first contestant to answer the question correctly will be our GRAND PRIZE WINNER and will receive our SURPRISE GRAND PRIZE! Whew! Now that that's done, let's get this show on the road! I'm gonna need 3 CONTESTANTS from the audience. And to help select them is my ASSISTANT, (INTRODUCE ASSISTANT WHO WALKS OUT ON STAGE.) O.K., (ASSISTANT'S NAME), you know what to do!

(ASSISTANT goes out in the audience and selects 3 CONTESTANTS, whom she leads to the CONTESTANTS' desk where they are seated.)

HOST/HOSTESS:

    Thank you, (ASSISTANT'S NAME).

ASSISTANT: (To HOST/HOSTESS) You're welcome.
    (Exit DOWNSTAGE LEFT)

HOST/HOSTESS:

    Now, ladies and gentlemen, we're going to find out who our wonderful CONTESTANTS are. Let's start with CONTESTANT NO. 1 to my right and nearest the audience. Tell us your name and a bit about yourself.

(CONTESTANT NO. 1 briefly introduces him/herself.)

HOST/HOSTESS:

    Thank you. And now CONTESTANT NO. 2 next to CONTESTANT NO. 1.

(CONTESTANT NO. 2 introduces him/herself.)

HOST/HOSTESS:

    And thank you very much. And CONTESTANT NO. 3, if you please.

(CONTESTANT NO. 3 introduces him/herself.)

HOST/HOSTESS:

    Thank you. And now let the game begin! CONTESTANTS, you have 3 categories from which you may select questions. The categories are: *ATHLETES/POLITICIANS/ CIVIL RIGHTS ACTIVISTS & MORE; GREAT AFRO-AMERICAN HEROINES; and ENTERTAINERS & WRITERS.* Are you ready?

(CONTESTANTS acknowledge that they are.)

HOST/HOSTESS (cont'd.):

    Good! Then I'll ask the first question. Remember to keep your hand on your buzzer/bell, and whoever responds/rings first, gets first crack at our question. Here we go!

(The game proceeds for 5 to 15 minutes at which time a bell rings, signaling the end of the PRELIMINARY ROUND.)

(REFER TO APPENDICES A, B, AND C: PRELIMINARY ROUND LIST OF QUESTIONS)

HOST/HOSTESS:

> Well, let's see. (NAME OF CONTESTANT) has the highest number of points with a total of (TOTAL NUMBER OF POINTS) in all. And (NAME OF CONTESTANT has the second highest total with (TOTAL NUMBER OF POINTS.) Well, (NAME OF 3RD CONTESTANT), we'd like to thank you for participating, and if you'll follow (ASSISTANT'S NAME) –

(ASSISTANT enters from STAGE LEFT and approaches the 3RD CONTESTANT.)

HOST/HOSTESS (cont'd.):

> -- she'll give you a Certificate acknowledging your participation in our first *AFRO-AMERICANS -- OUR PRIDE IS SHOWING GAME SHOW.* Once again, thank you.

(ASSISTANT leads CONTESTANT with Lowest Point Total OFFSTAGE. They exit STAGE LEFT.)

HOST/HOSTESS:

> (To remaining CONTESTANTS)
> Well, congratulations for making it to our GRAND PRIZE ROUND! In this round, I have in this envelope -- (Holds it up) --our GRAND PRIZE QUESTION worth 1,000 points! And the person who gets it right, is our GRAND PRIZE WINNER!

NOTE: *IT IS RECOMMENDED THAT THE HOST/HOSTESS HAVE AT LEAST 3-5 GRAND PRIZE QUESTIONS IN THE EVENT THAT NEITHER CONTESTANT IS ABLE TO ANSWER IT CORRECTLY.*

HOST/HOSTESS (cont'd.):

> In the unlikely event that neither is able to answer the question correctly, we have 2 additional questions that can be asked. If by chance neither question is answered correctly, then the CONTESTANT with the highest point total will be declared the GRAND PRIZE WINNER. In the event of a tie, both CONTESTANTS will be declared the CO-GRAND PRIZE WINNERS. So are you ready?

(CONTESTANTS acknowledge that they are.)

HOST/HOSTESS (cont'd.):

> O.K. So here's the moment everyone has been waiting for. (Raises the envelope again and this time, removes the question.) Please make sure your hand is on your bell/buzzer. (Pause) Here's the question.

(Reads the question)

(REFER TO APPENDIX D: GRAND PRIZE QUESTIONS LIST)

(One of the CONTESTANTS correctly answers the GRAND PRIZE QUESTION and is elated.)

HOST/HOSTESS:

> (Responding to the correct answer) That's right! And you're our GRAND PRIZE WINNER! Congratulations! (Walks over to the GRAND PRIZE WINNER and congratulates him/her) Congratulations! And thank you for participating. (ASSISTANT'S NAME) has your GRAND PRIZE for you.

(ASSISTANT brings out the gift and presents it to the winning CONTESTANT)

HOST/HOSTESS (cont'd.):

> Congratulations, (NAME OF GRAND PRIZE WINNER). And thank you, our studio audience,

HOST/HOSTESS (cont'd.):
> for being with us at our first, *AFRO-AMERICANS: OUR PRIDE IS SHOWING GAME SHOW!*

(Music plays softly in the background. SUGGESTED SONG: *LIFT EVERY VOICE AND SING*).

HOST/HOSTESS:
> (To AUDIENCE) If you would, please stand and sing our National Anthem, *LIFT EVERY VOICE AND SING*, with us.

(EVERYONE stands and sings.)

HOST/HOSTESS:
> (At the conclusion of *LIFT EVERY VOICE AND SING*) Thank you, ladies and gentlemen, and see you next year... same time ... same station! God bless, and good night/day.

THE END.

APPENDIX A:

PRELIMINARY ROUND LIST OF QUESTIONS

CATEGORY: ATHLETES/POLITICIANS/CIVIL RIGHTS ACTIVISTS & MORE

1. *THIS LITTLE LIGHT OF MINE* was the theme song of this brave Civil Rights Activist who is frequently quoted as having said, "I'm sick and tired of being sick and tired".

   Answer: FANNIE LOU HAMER   50 POINTS

2. Her refusal to give up her bus seat to a Caucasian is believed to be the spark that propelled the Civil Rights Movement forward -- full speed ahead.

   Answer: ROSA PARKS   100 POINTS

PRELIMINARY ROUND LIST OF QUESTIONS

CATEGORY: ATHLETES/POLITICIANS/CIVIL RIGHTS ACTIVISTS & MORE

3. This gentleman was an astronomer, mathematician and surveyor who built a wooden clock during the 18th century.

   Answer: BENJAMIN BANNEKER   150 POINTS

4. Name one of the Winningest Football Coaches in the history of the game. He served as Head Coach of the GRAMBLING STATE UNIVERSITY Tigers.

   Answer: EDDIE ROBINSON   200 POINTS

PRELIMINARY ROUND LIST OF QUESTIONS

CATEGORY: ATHLETES/POLITICIANS/CIVIL RIGHTS ACTIVISTS & MORE

5. She was a member of the Houston Comets, which is the First Championship Team of the WOMEN'S NATIONAL BASKETBALL ASSOCIATION (WNBA). In 1997 this phenomenal player was voted MOST VALUABLE PLAYER (MVP) of the Championship Game against the New York Liberty. Who is that player?

Answer: CYNTHIA COOPER   250 POINTS

APPENDIX B:

PRELIMINARY ROUND LIST OF QUESTIONS

CATEGORY: GREAT AFRO-AMERICAN HEROINES

1. Talk show host who has won numerous Emmy Awards. She appeared in the film, *THE COLOR PURPLE*, and owns her own production company, HARPO. Who is she?

   Answer: OPRAH WINFREY   50 POINTS

2. This grand diva and operatic soprano has performed in major opera houses throughout the world. She debuted at the New York Metropolitan Opera House in 1977. Extremely versatile as an artist, she has even performed with such jazz greats as Wynton and Branford Marsailles. Who is she?

   Answer: KATHLEEN BATTLE   100 POINTS

PRELIMINARY ROUND LIST OF QUESTIONS

CATEGORY: GREAT AFRO-AMERICAN HEROINES

3. "Nervy Lady" as she was known, this daring lady received the distinct honor of being the first licensed pilot of Afro-American ancestry. Who was this brave lady?

   Answer: BESSIE COLEMAN   150 POINTS

4. Who was the pioneer in cosmetology who popularized the straightening comb?

   Answer: MADAME C. J. WALKER   200 POINTS

5. Born in Portsmouth, Virginia in 1869, she was an opera singer who was known as the "First Negro prima donna".

   Answer: SISSIERETTA JONES   250 POINTS

APPENDIX C:

PRELIMINARY ROUND LIST OF QUESTIONS

CATEGORY: ENTERTAINERS & WRITERS

1. Recognized as the greatest jazz singer of all time whose music had a major impact on contemporary jazz as well as pop music. She was nicknamed *Lady Day*. Who was she?

Answer: BILLIE HOLIDAY   50 POINTS

2. This great "King" was posthumously featured on the re-recorded version of his smash hit, *UNFORGHTTABLE*, with his daughter, Natalie in the 1990s. Who was he?

Answer: NAT "KING" COLE   100 POINTS

PRELIMINARY ROUND LIST OF QUESTIONS

CATEGORY: ENTERTAINERS & WRITERS

3. What great Afro-American poet collaborated with R. Rosamond Johnson to create the National Black Anthem, *LIFT EVERY VOICE AND SING?*

Answer: JAMES WELDON JOHNSON   150 POINTS

4. Who is the essayist and author who wrote the novel, *THE COLOR PURPLE*, which was later made into a film by director Steven Spielberg in the mid-1980s and a Broadway musical in 2005?

Answer: ALICE WALKER   200 POINTS

PRELIMINARY ROUND LIST OF QUESTIONS

CATEGORY: ENTERTAINERS & WRITERS

5. This great composer, publisher, and promoter revolutionized Afro-American church music when he introduced gospel music in the late 1920s. Known as the *Father of Gospel*, who was he?

Answer: THOMAS A. DORSEY   250 POINTS

APPENDIX D:

GRAND PRIZE QUESTIONS LIST

1. In 1908 this Hall of Fame boxer became the First Afro-American to win the Heavyweight Championship Title. Who was he?

Answer: JACK JOHNSON

2. A true champion and trailblazer in Professional Women's Tennis, she won both the U.S. Open and the Wimbledon Tennis Tournaments in 1957 and 1958, which earned her the Number One ranking. Who was this grand dame of tennis?

Answer: ALTHEA GIBSON

GRAND PRIZE QUESTIONS LIST

3. A devout Baptist, this athlete once recognized as the world's fastest bicyclist, kept the Sabbath Day Holy by refusing to race on that day.

   Who was he?

   Answer: MAJOR TAYLOR

4. She was a member of the U.S. Space crew that ventured into outer space aboard the capsule *ENDEAVOR*. Who is this outstanding woman who is our first Afro-American astronaut?

   Answer: DR. MAE C. JEMISON

GRAND PRIZE QUESTIONS LIST

5. Author of her autobiographical book, *I KNOW WHY THE CAGED BIRD SINGS*, this author, educator, and actress was the Official Poet for the 1993 Inauguration of President William Jefferson Clinton.

   Answer: MAYA ANGELOU

6. This prestigious author won such accolades as the National Book Critics Award for *SONG OF SOLOMON* in 1977, the Pulitzer Prize for Fiction for *BELOVED* in 1987, and was the first Afro-American female to receive the Nobel Prize for Literature in 1993. Who is she?

   Answer: TONI MORRISON

GRAND PRIZE QUESTIONS LIST

7. The independent spirit of this strong-willed Harlem Renaissance writer led her to write such acclaimed books as *THEIR EYES WERE WATCHING GOD* and *MOSES, MAN OF THE MOUNTAIN*. Who was this daring and fearless soul?

Answer: ZORA NEALE HURSTON

8. Jazz vocalist whose career spanned more than fifty years. Blessed with an extraordinary vocal range, she was best known for her improvisational lyricism known as "scatting". Who is she?

Answer: ELLA FITZGERALD

GRAND PRIZE QUESTIONS LIST

9. She is the first female to be inducted into the Rock and Roll Hall of Fame and has won an unprecedented total of 15 Grammy Awards. Who is this undisputed *Queen Of Soul* who recorded the unforgettable hit, *RESPECT*?

Answer: ARETHA FRANKLIN

10. Who was one of the first Afro-American actors to obtain star status after making his first movie, *THE EAGLE'S NEST*, in 1914?

Answer: NOBLE JOHNSON

NOTE: *ALL GRAND PRIZE QUESTIONS ARE WORTH 1000 POINTS EACH.*

ABOUT THE AUTHOR

Zeretha Jenkins received her formal training at New York University's Tisch School of the Arts where she excelled as a writer. She's versatile as a playwright, screenwriter, and fiction writer.

Her plays, *AN EVERLASTING TRUTH* **and** *ILLUSION IN BLUE,* received staged readings at New York University, the Frank Silvera Writers' Workshop, and at the world-renowned Schomburg Center for Research on Black Culture in conjunction with the Frederick Douglass Creative Arts Center. *AN EVERLASTING TRUTH* was selected as one of the winning scripts in the prestigious Annual Writing Competition sponsored by *Writer's Digest Magazine*.

While demonstrating remarkable talent as an actress, director and most recently a producer, Zeretha continues to earn accolades for her writing in a variety of genres. Her creation of strong dramatic characters - particularly lead female characters — helped her script, ***AN EVERLASTING TRUTH***, win in the Script category of the prestigious Annual Writing Competition sponsored by *Writer's Digest Magazine*. She adapts fictional and non-fictional works for the stage and screen, and has even adapted one of her original plays, ***ILLUSION IN BLUE***, for the screen.

In terms of future projects, Zeretha is hard at work on another feature film script, a one-woman show, and another book -- a collection of inspirational short stories and dramatic works. As an entrepreneur, she owns and operates her own production company. Additional career goals include writing, directing, and producing future works for commercial theatre, television and film.

Contact Information:

Additional information regarding her books & bookings for speaking engagements may be obtained by contacting:

E.F.S. ENTERPRISES
P.O. BOX 7605
NEW YORK, NY 10116-7605
TEL: (212) 283-8899   (866) 202-4059
EMAIL: efsenterprises@hotmail.com
www.efs-enterprises.com
www.walkingbyfaithonline.com

ABOUT THE AUTHOR

Zeretha Jenkins received her formal training at New York University's Tisch School of the Arts where she excelled as a writer. She's versatile as a playwright, screenwriter, and fiction writer.

Her plays, ***AN EVERLASTING TRUTH* and *ILLUSION IN BLUE*,** received staged readings at New York University, the Frank Silvera Writers' Workshop, and at the world-renowned Schomburg Center for Research on Black Culture in conjunction with the Frederick Douglass Creative Arts Center. ***AN EVERLASTING TRUTH*** was selected as one of the winning scripts in the prestigious Annual Writing Competition sponsored by *Writer's Digest Magazine*.

While demonstrating remarkable talent as an actress, director and most recently a producer, Zeretha continues to earn accolades for her writing in a variety of genres. Her creation of strong dramatic characters - particularly lead female characters — helped her script, *AN EVERLASTING TRUTH,* win in the Script category of the prestigious Annual Writing Competition sponsored by *Writer's Digest Magazine*. She adapts fictional and non-fictional works for the stage and screen, and has even adapted one of her original plays, *ILLUSION IN BLUE,* for the screen.

In terms of future projects, Zeretha is hard at work on another feature film script, a one-woman show, and another book -- a collection of inspirational short stories and dramatic works. As an entrepreneur, she owns and operates her own production company. Additional career goals include writing, directing, and producing future works for commercial theatre, television and film.

Contact Information:

Additional information regarding her books & bookings for speaking engagements may be obtained by contacting:

E.F.S. ENTERPRISES
P.O. BOX 7605
NEW YORK, NY 10116-7605
TEL: (212) 283-8899   (866) 202-4059
EMAIL: efsenterprises@hotmail.com
www.efs-enterprises.com
www.walkingbyfaithonline.com

WALKING BY FAITH ORDER FORM

YES, I WANT TO EXPERIENCE THE THRILL OF WALKING BY FAITH...PLEASE SEND ME:

_____Walking By Faith: An Afro-American
   Trilogy $12.95

_____Walking By Faith: An Afro-American
   Trilogy And More $18.95

_____Walking By Faith: Fact Or Fiction $21.95

Please send orders to the following address and enclose $5.00 for Priority Mail ($15.00 outside the U.S.):

E.F.S. ENTERPRISES
P.O. BOX 7605
NEW YORK, NY 10116-7605
TEL: (212) 283-8899   (866) 202-4059
EMAIL: efsenterprises@hotmail.com
www.efs-enterprises.com
www.walkingbyfaithonline.com

www.ingramcontent.com/pod-product-compliance
Lightning Source LLC
Chambersburg PA
CBHW051707040426
42446CB00008B/768